MIND HACKING

25 advanced persuasion techniques

Introduction

This is a unique book.

What we will see in this book is a very particular and transversal topic, which can be applied to sales, copywriting, marketing of any kind.

Persuasion is critical to the effectiveness of what we do, and in this book, we will see 25 Advanced persuasion techniques that will give you access to shortcuts for the customer's mind.

You can apply these techniques on different occasions, from the simple copywriting text to the drafting of a marketing plan for your company.

It is also interesting to know these strategies to be able to recognize them when they are applied to us: these are techniques known until now only by the largest companies that will give access to incredible results.

PS: We've all been there. By reading this text, you will recognize different methods that have also been applied to you, to make you believe or buy something.

There is nothing wrong with this: you have not been deceived.

These techniques work thanks to internal mechanisms of our mind, and very often we cannot block them or recognize them when they are used.

Use this in your favor: now that you have this book, you will be able to structure your work so as to apply these strategies to maximize your results.

Finally, I ask you to use these techniques for positive purposes.

Let's be honest, in the world, these manipulation strategies are often used to deceive people. Because they work, and those who know them are tempted to take the shortest way to make them bear fruit.

However, a company that sells poor quality products or services with these persuasion strategies will be able to sell a lot, but will not have satisfied customers.
It is not a sustainable long-term plan.

Index

Create affinity

The first technique we're going to see is one of the best known.

We often see it used, but we may never have stopped to think specifically about what it is: it is the construction of a system of affinity and empathy with the customer.

What is meant by affinity? It is simply a matter of finding and highlighting similarities between us and our client. The goal is to allow the customer to identify with us. This creates a relationship of trust that allows us to take part, indirectly, in its decisions.

A very simple example of this technique is found in some telesales: the testimonials speak, before the product, of their problems and their difficulties, which will then go to resolve with the product that the advertiser wants to sell.

The purpose of these scenes is to allow target customers to identify themselves in one of the testimonials, to make them exclaim "I too have this problem!" And the direct consequence will be "I too can solve it like this."

Abdication of responsibility

What often stops people buying is the stance, the responsibility that a wrong choice can result: the difficulty in justifying to others but especially towards you any waste of money.

This is the real strength of the affinity relationship that we can create with the customer. We, or our testimonial, there We assume this responsibility instead of the customer. The customer, coming to trust us, entrusts us with the responsibility of choosing the purchase.

And we already know what to choose!

If something goes wrong, the customer can get rid of guilt. His reaction will no longer be that of a person who has made a wrong purchase, but that of a person victim of wrong advice - this is why this strategy, although so powerful, must always be combined with a very high-quality product.

This abdication of responsibility happens all the time: just think how often we don't check the prices we are offered, *trusting* that the person we deal with is proposing us, if not a low price, at least fair?

This also happens when, for example, we rely on a lawyer to safeguard our interests. How do we know, if we are not experts in the field, that he is really acting in our interest?

We do not know. But it is convenient to assume that this is the case: the alternative is to undertake the study path that led the lawyer to be who he is now; a decidedly impractical solution.

The first step is, therefore, to find affinity with the client: let us take an interest in him, and see how we can build it.
We can also use this technique in copywriting: let's start from our target to understand who are the people who will read our text, and consequently analyze what are the points on which we can leverage.

What interests the customer?

Ok, so we need to see what the points are in common between us and the customer. But not all points are important in the same way: having brown hair is certainly not an affinity that we can use to leverage on his mind.

According to Dan Kennedy, the subjects that interest people are simple, and they are always the same.

- Family
- Work
- Interests
- Money

In this order.

And this is the order we should follow to start a discussion that will lead us to create an affinity relationship.

The first thing is always the family. More for women than for men, but in general it is statistically the topic that people care about most.

Then we can take an interest in employment. What do they do in life? What role do they have in their company, and how does this shape their day?

We continue: we now move on to free time. If we identify a hobby, a sport or any common recreational interest, we can talk about this. Common interests are extremely effective, and it is relatively easy to build affinities in this way: it is sufficient to be prepared on some basic topics - such as football, in Italy, to create a relationship with the vast majority of people.

Finally, we move on to talk about money, politics, the economy. It is important that this point be the last to talk about: before making an economic request, or any kind of commitment to our interlocutor, we must have created an affinity in the family, in work, and in interests.

This will incredibly increase our chances of success.

Indirect affinity

Do we have points in common with the interlocutor?
It is not a real problem. We cannot expect to have points in common with all people, in all the necessary subjects.

One trick we can use, however, is indirect affinity.
We use points in common with other people we know! It sounds incredible, but it really works.

"Do you have a daughter? Even my sister has one, now I'm looking for a photo. "
A phrase of this type, although it cannot create a direct affinity, serves the same

purpose and, incredibly, does not diminish the effectiveness of the affinity connection we are creating.

Transparency and intrigue

The purpose of this is to convey transparency: we must be transparent to our interlocutor, to allow him to trust us.

In particular, if we are a public figure, it is useful to be transparent with what are our faults or otherwise they could be perceived as such.

In fact, very often these traits are not really negative, except when we try to hide them. This works particularly well in politics: aspects of the character's private life are often communicated in a negative light if this is done by opponents.
This is obviously not possible if the politician in question has always been transparent in this regard: if everything is known, there is nothing to discover. In this case, we are sure that nothing can be used against us.

On the contrary: these aspects (we can say, improperly, *defects*) can create relationships of affinity, as we have seen previously.

People will identify with us if they are related to us in this respect. And, even if for them this is a cause for shame, it should not be for us; it is important that they know that they will not be judged differently on the basis of these aspects, because they are simply shared also by their interlocutor.

If on the one hand, transparency plays in our favor, on the other we also want to keep a veil of mystery about our person to intrigue people.

Creating an aura of mystery around our figure leads people to want to know more about us.

This keeps them "around" us, and gives us the opportunity to meet them, to talk, to communicate and to sell.

The solution is, therefore, to balance the two things, transparency, and mystery, and exploit both these aspects.

If we are 100% transparent, people will lose interest quickly and forget us. On the contrary, if we are too mysterious, people will not trust us.

Flattery and licenses

To hear the people the desire to be with us, and make them feel our lack when we are not, we must ensure that they feel better when we are with them.

Each person's hidden desire is to be - or to feel - better than others.

What we need to do is give them this permission. They must understand that we know, and that we agree, that they are better.

Not good people: people better than others, or at least most of the others.

We must, therefore, give them the license to feel in a way that they normally do not feel free to feel, to think in a way that they reasonably believe does not have the right to do.

But with us, they can, and we understand them.

This is also true in many other contexts: helping people to justify themselves in their comparisons is extremely useful.
It may seem trivial, but many people have this problem: they hear something that they rationally believe is wrong.
Or they would like to behave in a way that their mind knows is not right.

If, when they are with us, they are allowed to be like they want to be, to do what they want to do, we can be sure that they will look for our company in the future.

Everyone wants to be special

A special case of this strange permission system is the lure.
People like to be considered special.

This aspect recalls a text by Blair Warren, which lists 6 steps that are followed to request the participation of a person in a cause. This system relies on the need for these people to be considered - by others but also by themselves - special.

1.   Explain the situation in its entirety and make it clear what the problem you want to solve

2.   Explain the role the donor can play in this situation

3.   Emphasize the importance of this role, so that you can understand, indirectly, that the person is important to your cause

4.   Explain why you believe the person you are talking to is right for that role

5.   Ask if you can count on him

A particular technique that can be used is *conditional flattery.*

It's very simple: a person is complimented, but this is only valid if he agrees to do what we want.

An example is a phrase like this:
"We know we can count on you because you are a good person who cares about this issue."

Create a ritual

This is very common in ... religions!
Creating a ritual is an incredibly effective way to retain people and make them feel the need to be there, to participate.

This thing works. It has been used, perhaps purely by chance, over the centuries. Just think of the importance of parties, ceremonies, events that have been made real rituals.
We don't even realize it: we want to participate, we don't know why, but we know we want to be there.

This behavior has been taught to us since we were children: just think of the school; the uniforms, the strict schedules, the interval. We felt part of something.

We make people feel part of something, and they will continue to want to feel that

23

way. It doesn't matter if it's something stupid: most religious rituals are difficult to justify rationally, but they work.

Creating a ritual guarantees that people continue to follow us, because the detachment from this ritual, which they are now used to, is something they want to avoid.

Symbolism

Linked to the importance of rituals is that of symbolism.
This is a simple concept, but it is often ignored or not applied properly.

Just think of the most valuable brand in the world: Apple.
Apple presents itself, in many ways, as much more than an electronics company.

Owning an iPhone does not mean having the ability to call, send messages, and all the new features that other manufacturers sponsor.

Owning an iPhone is a symbol, and that's enough.

Apple does not promote the features, functionalities or specifications of its phones: it is sufficient to let people know that there is a new iPhone.

Symbolism does the rest.

Demonstrations

The demonstrations are very important. We think of telesales - none of us probably want to look like teleshopping, yet these are designed and structured to sell, and they really work.

What we don't know, and that doesn't matter even if we know it, is that very often these demonstrations are distorted.

They could also represent the product in a case of real use, but for these tests, the ideal conditions were created to obtain the desired result.
Moreover, very often, especially if we have the opportunity to record these demos, we will happen to do repeated tests. And of course, the final version will be the one with the best result, not necessarily the most realistic!

We, therefore, remember: we prove that our product works. It doesn't matter if the proof is mounted ad-hoc, and it doesn't matter if we fear it can be discovered too easily.

People want to believe that what we sell really works, so they can solve their problem.
We must give them the material they need to believe it.

The numbers count

It is easy to believe that if a large number of people believe in something, this is true.
It is not logical or correct reasoning, yet it works. Very often we also do it unintentionally.

Therefore, if a large number of people have bought, or used, one of our products, this must be of good quality.

It is therefore very useful to indicate these numbers in the sale. Let's think about how many times we read phrases like "*Chosen by over one million customers.*"
This means nothing, except that the company is able to sell the product. However, sentences of this type are extremely effective and create what is called *social proof*.

What is interesting is the total absence of logic in statements of this kind.

We know that the product has been chosen by one million customers. But is a million customers a lot or a little?

The reference market could be composed of 5 million people as of 5 billion. They could have presented the product to 100 million people to convince then only 1% of the purchase.

We, therefore, understand that the number, without a context around it, is simply meaningless. Yet it is extremely effective because it *seems* *like* a high number.

Another important aspect to consider is that the number is more important than the action: if one million customers have purchased our product and, of these, 100,000 still uses it after 10 years, indicating the second digit logically has more meaning important: it suggests that these people are very convinced of the value of the product and demonstrate it, using it after a certain period of time.

However, the number is lower.
The fact is, the number counts more than the context. If we can then formulate a text with a larger number, the result will be better; it doesn't matter if the concept is less interesting.

I told you

In this chapter, we will see how to always be right and gain the trust of our customers even on forecasts for which they should not trust us.

The principle behind this logic is that on which horoscopes, astrologers and in general all these people who say they can predict the future are based.
The same is also true in more formal environments, from which we would expect a more serious and responsible behavior (Wrong! Actually we assume that this is the case because we trust).

The principle is very simple: if I guess once, it doesn't matter how many times I did wrong.
We can make dozens of predictions on the value of shares, cryptocurrencies, on the

expansion or contraction of markets, on trends and much more.

If even one of these is true, we will all be known as "the one who predicted the X boom."

It matters little if we have also foreseen another ten booms that did not actually take place.

Moreover, the same can also be done in the dimension of time. We may have been extremely successful for a short period of time. It doesn't matter, let's use that.

Were our forecasts correct and effective in March 2017? Let's take March 2017 as an example of our abilities.

We decide what to write in our sales letter, or what to talk about in our event. We, therefore, choose, without problems, the arguments that bring us the most advantage - our competitors do the same.

A particularly interesting example is that of gambling. Think of the Superenalotto: sometimes you hear of millionaire winnings, and many people are tempted.
What is not said, but that we all know well, is how much capital players spend to create these jackpots.

The number of people losing to the Superenalotto or the number of games that do not bring substantial victories is not advertised. We only talk about the positive aspect, when we all know rationally that the other side of the coin has a much greater economic weight.

The authority

Who writes, sends, says or in any way communicates the message, is extremely important.
The person or company from whom everything starts counts.

Choosing a good source for ours is fundamental. The idea is to be ourselves the source we need: in this case, the people who receive the message trust us, give value to our communications and therefore pay particular attention to what we say.

How to steal authority

But this is not always the case.
Especially if we are starting out, we cannot expect the recipient of our message to

listen to us. Because he doesn't know who we are.

In this case, we need to take the authority of someone else.
The positive note is that there are several ways to do it, and it is extremely easy.

We can hire testimonials or influencers to promote our brand. The unconscious reasoning that potential customers will do is that if a service is produced and promoted by an authoritative person, then it must be quality.
And this allows us to become authoritative ourselves in our sector.

And so far it may seem obvious. What is not considered, however, is that the medium through which communication takes place also counts.
Being on TV, for example, gives us very important credibility. And it is not only due

to the number of people reached but also to the impression we give of ourselves.

The same happens with trade magazines: if we are published on Forbes, it doesn't matter who the journalist who wrote about us is. There is transferred authority from the magazine itself because this is positively evaluated by readers.

It is also interesting to note that the same transfer of authority takes place with paid advertisements: being on Forbes because a journalist wrote about us is extremely difficult, while anyone can be there by purchasing advertising space. Yet the effectiveness is the same!

We and them

A further strategy, often used in politics or in the social sphere, is that of dividing the world into two factions.

Good and bad, beautiful and ugly, honest and dishonest. It doesn't matter if the type of division makes sense or not, nor does it matter if there are more factions or even none.

Dividing people between "us and them" is a great way to create a sense of belonging.

A very effective strategy to achieve this is to create an enemy. We can identify a person, an opponent or a competitor, and exploit it to our advantage, presenting ourselves as the saviors of our customers towards this person.

It is important that this enemy is identified as a single entity. Let's say for example "we and them", not "us, group 2, group 3, etc." Similarly, we talk about "us and the competition," not about "us, the competitor 1, competitor 2" and so on.

This aspect is fundamental because we must present ourselves as able to help, to *save*, our listeners. We should not present ourselves as one of the alternatives, but as the only choice to avoid *something very bad*.

Buying resistance

We now introduce the concept of resistance threshold. What is it?
It's simple: in order for a person to move forward towards the purchase, it is necessary for her to overcome various barriers that tend to hold her in place.

For example, we opt for the following: our system for acquiring customers consists of an advertisement on Facebook that leads to a page that asks for an email, after 4 emails we try to close the sale.

The first step for the user is to click on one of our advertisements: relatively low threshold, so we can expect a good percentage of people to do it (compatible with the statistics of the medium).

The second step is to insert an email. This is private data, which some people tend not to leave easily. So the threshold is slightly higher; however, the fact that the person has clicked on the advertisement and is there to see our page is a sign of interest.

We can raise this threshold further, if we deem it appropriate, asking in addition to the email also other information such as name and surname.

After that, our lead will receive our emails. In this case, we have an advantage because by default it will not be removed from the list (there is a threshold of "annoyance" that it can bear). However, we must also make sure that you read our emails to get to the purchase.

Finally, we want you to end up buying by reading the text of our last mail.

We can see these thresholds as steps: a higher step is more difficult to climb but puts us in a position of advantage.

If on the page where we ask for the email address, we also ask for the name, we risk losing a part of our potential contacts. On the other hand, the contacts we end up receiving are the ones really interested in our product, and it's easier for them to end up buying.

We must, therefore, structure our plan so as not to place the customer in front of thresholds, insurmountable steps, but we must not even simplify the process too much and not require an investment in terms of time and attention on his part: if we do not have his own be careful and not even willing to read our emails, how do we expect you to buy?

Tip: if we use the telephone in our business, a pre-recorded message represents a much lower threshold than the interaction with a person.

Proceed by steps

But what are these steps, these steps that the potential customer must climb?

1.   Possibilities: it is necessary to let the potential customer know that there is the possibility of doing what we propose, or that our product simply exists.

2.   Benefit: we must now make it clear what the benefit of our product is, or the advantage that the buyer will have after having purchased it.

3.   Reachability: we must then make it clear that it is possible to really achieve the result - not as a bet (a lottery), but as a real possibility that we are offering to our customers

4.   Personal possibility: ok, it can be done. But can I do it myself? Even if I'm poor? Even if I'm low? Even if I

live in the countryside? We must take away all these doubts from our potential customer so that he can identify with our proposal

5. Difference: if the customer already has negative experiences with our competitors, we must explain why it will be different with us.

We must defeat the skepticism that created the one who came before us, and at the same time create it towards our competitors

6. Personal benefit: it is different from the generic benefit. We have to make our customer think about what will happen after buying our product. Not only what will he buy, but also how his life will change

7. Timeliness: ok, then you must buy it. Wait, you have to buy it NOW. We must provide valid reasons

why taking time is not wise. In this case, we can also integrate a concept of scarcity, as we have seen.

8.   The moral: ok it's all nice, I can do it. But will I do it? Many people are blocked, involuntarily, from what they believe to be right or wrong, lawful, and unlawful.

It is not a question of legality: obviously, we have to sell legal products and services. It is a problem of preconceptions, which we must dismantle or guide towards the direction that can allow the client to achieve his goals. Possibly passing by us.

Being aggressive?

Our first goal is to have our contact accept more information.
In fact, if we are excessively aggressive with the promotion before the potential customer has decided to learn more, we risk being too aggressive and making the customer "close."

We must, therefore, wait, and start the most aggressive sale only after the potential customer has accepted and shown a minimum of interest in knowing what we have to offer.

This is very evident in door-to-door sales, which are not widespread: the seller's first goal is not to start talking about the product and what it can do for the buyer, but it is to interest the potential buyer enough to accept learn more.

The same happens in online sales. For this reason, we use lead generation, relatively low-cost contacts that we can then educate, usually via email.

The final goal is that of selling, but we must not start from there: we make the customer interested in the product so that it is than he who wants to know more about it.

The false alternative

People like to be in control. Or at least believe you have it.

This strategy consists of placing the person in the situation of having a choice; the trick is that we create this situation.
You will still believe that you have chosen, but will have chosen by force, one of the alternatives that we have decided before - both must be positive options for us.

What kind of alternative can we offer our customers to make sure they have options that always play in our favor?

Here are three variables we can work on:
-    Product selection, when we simply offer two different products (or a product sold in a different format, for example with a bonus)

- Choice of time, for example, the customer can choose to receive the service now or have it within three months
- Choice of benefits, when the customer may need an additional service that may be more expensive, but even the basic one is fine for us - after all, pay for it!

Greedy is OK

We can choose different levers to motivate people to buy and take action.
One of the most important is greed.

People like to save or earn money, there is little to say.
And offering discounts or free products is an extremely effective method to attract potential customers and make them aware of our product.

It matters little if the discount we are offering is not credible or plausible. A discount of 70% would be excessive for most of the products in circulation if you do not *cheat* on the original price. But this is not a problem: buyers do not care if the original price is different from the day before; most buyers won't even notice.

This is what happens at Christmas time or near events like black Friday.

People care about saving so much and taking a high-value home. The fact is that we decide the starting price!

A product of € 1000 discounted by 80% has a perceived value of € 1000, while a product of € 200 that is not discounted remains a product of € 200.
As in many other examples we have seen, the rational component has very limited importance.

Part of this strategy is the provision of free services. For example, free shipping in online purchases.

Rationally, it is obvious that the cost of shipping is included in the price of the product. No salesman would be stupid enough to forget about it. Yet offering free shipping provides an incredible boost to sales.

We, therefore, take advantage of this magic word. As usual, it doesn't matter if it makes sense or not!

New is always better

In the same way as "free," even "new" is a word we can use to push people to buy.

It happened to us all: who should buy the latest fashion clothing, who should have the new iPhone model, etc.

The longer the wait, the greater the expectations for novelty, the easier it will be to complete the sale.
It doesn't matter if the new product is interesting, better or useful, there will be those who buy it just because it's new.

The purchase of a new product that we have craved for so long is a satisfaction, but this feeling starts to fade quickly, and we soon need a new product.

The ego of the customer

This technique relies on the social position of our client.
People continually confront each other, whether this makes sense or not.

This approach is widely used in companies that manage a sales force: rankings are always drawn up and prizes are awarded to the best sellers. When these are removed, the performances of all the sellers are lowered, not only those of the best.

The same also happens in the private sphere: we want to have that extra thing, the car, the pool, which our neighbors don't have. And when we have it, the same thing happens to them: in a short time the whole neighborhood ends up buying what we thought would have distinguished us.

The social status that our product can confer is very important and can lead us to many sales because our customers will like the fact that they can somehow feel superior to their friends, their colleagues, their neighbors, etc.

Furthermore, this technique goes very well with the rituals and symbolism we talked about a little while ago: just think of the ritual of an award ceremony or a cup or brooch that symbolizes our victory.
The effectiveness of these awards is that they can prove to be better than other people, and everyone can do it at least in a very specific field. The desire to be considered the best motivates and motivates people to do their best.

Sense of urgency

The fear of losing an opportunity is often stronger than the interest in the opportunity itself.
This concept may seem counterintuitive, but it is true and demonstrated.

Just think of how many occasions you play on the concept of scarcity: tickets for a concert by a famous singer will end right away, and if we're undecided we run the risk of buying them anyway because we don't have time to think about it too much.
The same reasoning is applied to limited edition products, which always have a greater appeal. It matters little if the limited edition is actually composed of millions of copies.

This concept is particularly strong when combined with a discount, as we saw earlier: if this discount is only valid for a limited time, it will be much easier to convince our leaders to buy. This is why Amazon, as well as much other e-commerce, always communicates when the product is about to end, and why the famous *flash offers* are so effective.

Destabilize the customer

Very often, the customer does not believe he needs our help.

During the information phase of the client, we must, therefore, instill in him also different doubts. He must come to doubt himself and his ability to successfully complete his work or achieve his goal.

And very often it really is. Let us imagine working with an entrepreneur who leads a successful company: for a person in his situation it is easy to think of being able to manage all aspects of his company, and therefore he will believe he does not need our advice.

The reality may be that his company, although well managed, could have achieved even better results with a different approach, or that the growth that makes him so sure of himself is actually slowing down, or that he is simply always positive, but less positive of the competition (therefore it is in an expanding market, and its company grows more slowly than the market, so it is actually losing shares even if the turnover increases).

The same can be done in many other ways and contexts. The key is, therefore, to make our potential customer think we need us: otherwise the decision is already made, and it is a "no."

(False) assumptions

We are literally full of beliefs, which are rooted within us. Let's take any topic: all we know about it is actually our opinion.
Ok, sometimes these opinions are formed on the basis of facts, but very often it is not so simple.

However, it doesn't matter: the important thing is to know how to recognize them and exploit them in our favor.
For example, it is much easier to sell a security system to a paranoid person than to another person who tends to feel very safe.
Whether this paranoia is justified or not does, it not matter: even if it were, it would be very difficult to make the second person change his mind - much more difficult than looking   for new customers   paranoid elsewhere.

When we try to define our client in detail, therefore, we keep in mind his beliefs, what he has spent in life and how this can provide him with the conditions for the future, the bases on which he will make future decisions.

Familiarity

In this chapter, we will see a very important concept: that of familiarity.

It is much easier for people to reason by referring to products, models, and concepts they already know.
Referring to something that is known, allows us not only to make ourselves
understood more quickly but also to create a connection between us and the other party.

Instead of referring to abstract discourses, therefore, it is advisable to be practical and speak with real examples and analogies that people know.
The effort to understand something new is, for many people, excessive. And they will unintentionally stop listening to us, making all our communication useless if they understand that what we are saying is

different from what they are used to. Moreover, they live well even this way.

The idea is yours

You have to find ways to get the customer to think about what you want. But he doesn't have to notice it, it must seem a natural process.
There are different ways to do this, and they all work on the lack of logic in some arguments.

People are used to making connections that are often unmotivated, yet they seem rational.
For example, we tend to believe that a well-dressed person in a suit and tie has more power. In reality, it is not necessarily so.

Yet, in sales, it is shown that this type of clothing really produces better results.
The same can apply to any type of assumption that people tend to do in an automatic way: let's think about it, let's try

to find a logical connection between the starting point and the point of arrival.

If it is not there, we have found an element that we can use in our favor to make people understand something we don't really say - and that can be true or not.

The magic word

There is a magic word that gives credibility and reinforces any statement.
This word is "why."

Several scientific tests have been made in this regard, such as the famous experiment of the printer queue: in an office, 94% of people are willing to give us a precedence in the queue at the photocopier, if in the sentence to ask them we say "why." Otherwise, this percentage drops to 60%.

The interesting thing, though, is not this.
It turns out, in fact, that what is said after the "why" does not matter.
The same test was repeated with these sentences:
- "Because I'm late for a meeting"
- "Because I have to make photocopies"

The second sentence is practically useless. It does not add information, not a reason for the urgency and why this person should pass us by.

Guess what is the success rate of the second sentence?

94%, exactly like the first one.

The word "why" is simply magical. Let's use it as much as possible, even when what comes next is meaningless.
It is "why" that matters, not why.

Hopes and fears

This technique is extremely powerful and can be applied to both physical products and services, both in B2B and in B2C.

People tend to believe what they hope for. And they hope not to make what they fear to happen.

The desire to make a purchase is as strong as it is important for the person, the thing that he risks losing if he does not proceed with the purchase.

A simple example is the burglar alarm: we don't really care that it sounds when someone enters the house. Or rather, he has to do it, but that's not why we buy it.
We buy it because we want to avoid losing our possessions, so for the hope of defeating our fear.

Time investment

There is direct proportionality between the time we spend with our lead and its probability of finalizing the purchase.

And the more time they spend with us, the more they will be satisfied after buying.

This obviously applies to live, but also to online sales. We record videos or write long articles: if we keep them interesting, the potential customer will have invested a great deal of time in us. After spending hours, days or months reading our articles, watching our videos, they will have no choice but to buy.

Otherwise, they would have lost all this time!

This aspect is also extremely valid for increasing the price of our product, so it is important to be extremely careful with the content we disseminate.

Disclaimer

All registered trademarks and logos mentioned in this book belong to their respective owners.

The author of this book does not claim or declare any rights to these trademarks, which are mentioned only for educational purposes.